# SACREDSPACE

for Advent and the Christmas Season
2012-2013

# SACREDSPACE

for Advent and the Christmas Season
2012-2013

December 2, 2012, to January 6, 2013

from the website www.sacredspace.ie
The Irish Jesuits

ave maria press AmP notre dame, indiana

# acknowledgment

The publisher would like to thank Brian Grogan, S.J., for his kind assistance in making this book possible. Correspondence with the Sacred Space team can be directed to feedback@sacredspace.ie or to www.sacredspace.ie, where comments or suggestions related to the book will always be welcome.

Unless otherwise noted, the Scripture quotations contained herein are from the *New Revised Standard Version* Bible, copyright © 1989 by the Division of Christian Education of the National Council of the Churches of Christ in the United States of America. Used by permission. All rights reserved.

Advent retreat by John Callahan, S.J.; used with permission.

Published under license from Michelle Anderson Publishing Pty Ltd., Australia.

Founded in 1865, Ave Maria Press is a ministry of the United States Province of Holy Cross.

www.avemariapress.com

ISBN-10: 1-59471-295-6 ISBN-13: 978-1-59471-295-1

Cover design by Andy Wagoner.

Text design by Kristen Hornyak Bonelli.

Printed and bound in the United States of America.

# contents

# how to use this booklet

———

We invite you to make a sacred space in your day and spend ten minutes praying here and now, wherever you are, with the help of a prayer guide and scripture chosen specially for each day of Advent and the Christmas season. Every place is a sacred space so you may wish to have this book in your desk at work or available to be picked up and read at any time of the day, whilst traveling or on your bedside table, a park bench . . . Remember that God is everywhere, all around us, constantly reaching out to us, even in the most unlikely situations. When we know this, and with a bit of practice, we can pray anywhere.

The following pages will guide you through a session of prayer stages:

Something to think and pray about each day this week

The Presence of God

Freedom

Consciousness

The Word (leads you to the daily scripture and
provides help with the text)

Conversation

Conclusion

It is most important to come back to these
pages each day of the week as they are an in-
tegral part of each day's prayer and lead to the
scripture and inspiration points.

Although written in the first person, the
prayers are for "doing" rather than for reading
out. Each stage is a kind of exercise or meditation aimed at helping you to get in touch with
God and God's presence in your life. We hope
that you will join the many people around the
world praying with us in our sacred space.

# The Presence of God

Bless all who worship you, almighty God,
from the rising of the sun to its setting:
from your goodness enrich us,
by your love inspire us,
by your Spirit guide us,
by your power protect us,
in your mercy receive us,
now and always.

# december 2–8, 2012

Something to think and pray about each day this week:

## Seeking the Joy of Christmas

Psychiatrists say they are at their busiest in the weeks leading up to Christmas. The feast stirs up anxieties linked to memories of childhood and relationships within the family. It pushes us to difficult decisions about sending invitations, cards, or gifts. No wonder people talk about "getting over Christmas." But our real friends do not judge us by those decisions. They like us to be calm and contented in ourselves, with a clean emotional palate so that we can enter into and taste other people's joys.

## The Presence of God

Lord, help me to be fully alive to your holy presence.
Enfold me in your love.
Let my heart become one with yours.

## Freedom

Many countries are at this moment suffering the agonies of war.
I bow my head in thanksgiving for my freedom.
I pray for all prisoners and captives.

## Consciousness

At this moment, Lord, I turn my thoughts to You.
I will leave aside my chores and preoccupations.
I will take rest and refreshment in your presence, Lord.

## The Word

The Word of God comes down to us through the scriptures.

May the Holy Spirit enlighten my mind and
my heart to respond to the gospel teachings.
(Please turn to your scripture on the following
pages. Inspiration points are there should you
need them. When you are ready, return here to
continue.)

## Conversation

Sometimes I wonder what I might say
if I were to meet You in person, Lord.
I might say "Thank You, Lord" for always
being there for me.
I know with certainty there were times when
you carried me.
When through your strength, I got through
the dark times in my life.

## Conclusion

Glory be to the Father, and to the Son, and to
the Holy Spirit,
As it was in the beginning, is now and ever
shall be,
World without end. Amen.

### Sunday 2nd December,
### First Sunday of Advent       Mark 13:33–37

Beware, keep alert; for you do not know when the time will come. It is like a man going on a journey, when he leaves home and puts his slaves in charge, each with his work, and commands the doorkeeper to be on the watch. Therefore, keep awake—for you do not know when the master of the house will come, in the evening, or at midnight, or at cockcrow, or at dawn, or else he may find you asleep when he comes suddenly. And what I say to you I say to all: Keep awake."

- Jesus' message and life was to make a difference and save the world. That's the call—to do the world a world of good. Stay awake—see how you can make someone else's life that bit better. We need to believe that each of us can make a difference to our families, to the neighborhood, to the school. One way is to keep in touch with God.

- Advent can be a time to make sure—through prayer, Mass, through helping the very poor—that we keep in touch with God. We allow God's grace and care to flow through us.

### Monday 3rd December,
### St. Francis Xavier       1 Corinthians 9:19, 22–23

For though I am free with respect to all, I have made myself a slave to all, so that I might win more of them. To the weak I became weak, so that I might win the weak. I have become all things to all people, that I might by all means save some. I do it all for the sake of the gospel, so that I may share in its blessings.

- Like Francis Xavier, I bring myself to God for healing, strength, and encouragement. I listen for the words that God has for me.

- As I bring my desires to God, I ask for the focus that I need to serve God wholeheartedly.

**Tuesday 4th December**     Luke 10:21–24

At that same hour Jesus rejoiced in the Holy Spirit and said, "All things have been handed over to me by my Father; and no one knows who the Son is except the Father, or who the Father is except the Son and anyone to whom the Son chooses to reveal him." Then turning to the disciples, Jesus said to them privately, "Blessed are the eyes that see what you see! For I tell you that many prophets and kings desired to see what you see, but did not see it, and to hear what you hear, but did not hear it."

- To rejoice in the Holy Spirit is to be aware of the Father's infinite and unconditional love poured out on me. Are there moments in my life when I have felt such love? What may be preventing me from experiencing such love today?

- Jesus says, "Blessed are the eyes that see what you see." The disciples are "blessed" because, in Jesus, they are beginning to recognize the long awaited Messiah. Do I ever count my blessings, thanking God for the gifts of life and love?

## Wednesday 5th December        Isaiah 25:6–9

On this mountain the LORD of hosts will make for all peoples a feast of rich food, a feast of well-aged wines, of rich food filled with marrow, of well-aged wines strained clear. And he will destroy on this mountain the shroud that is cast over all peoples, the sheet that is spread over all nations; he will swallow up death forever. Then the Lord GOD will wipe away the tears from all faces, and the disgrace of his people he will take away from all the earth, for the LORD has spoken. It will be said on that day, Lo, this is our God; we have waited for him, so that he might save us. This is the LORD for whom we have waited; let us be glad and rejoice in his salvation.

- Do I dare to hope for a great and glorious day in the future when all our tears will be wiped away, when all my shortcomings and failings will count for nothing and I will rest, joyful, in God's loving presence?

- How does the Lord's promise resonate with me? Does it excite me and confirm my deepest hopes?

Does it seem to go against the grain of my experience and leave me confused and unsure?

- Can I bring what is in my heart to the Lord, in this time of prayer?

**Thursday 6th December      Matthew 7:21, 24–27**

Jesus said to the people, "Not everyone who says to me, 'Lord, Lord,' will enter the kingdom of heaven, but only the one who does the will of my Father in heaven. Everyone then who hears these words of mine and acts on them will be like a wise man who built his house on rock. The rain fell, the floods came, and the winds blew and beat on that house, but it did not fall, because it had been founded on rock. And everyone who hears these words of mine and does not act on them will be like a foolish man who built his house on sand. The rain fell, and the floods came, and the winds blew and beat against that house, and it fell—and great was its fall!"

- Lord, you never let me forget that love is shown in deeds, not words or feelings. I could fill notebooks with resolutions and in the end be further from you.

- As William James put it: "A resolution that is a fine flame of feeling allowed to burn itself out without appropriate action, is not merely a lost opportunity, but a bar to future action."

### Friday 7th December      Matthew 9:27–31

As Jesus went on from there, two blind men followed him, crying loudly, "Have mercy on us, Son of David!" When he entered the house, the blind men came to him; and Jesus said to them, "Do you believe that I am able to do this?" They said to him, "Yes, Lord." Then he touched their eyes and said, "According to your faith let it be done to you." And their eyes were opened. Then Jesus sternly ordered them, "See that no one knows of this." But they went away and spread the news about him throughout that district.

- In matters of faith, we are all blind in some way. But if I allow Jesus to touch my heart, he will help me see more clearly the path I should follow.

- The blind men had faith in Jesus' power of healing. Do I ever experience the inner healing power of God?

## Saturday 8th December,
## The Immaculate Conception of
## the Blessed Virgin Mary      Luke 1:30–33

The angel said to her, "Do not be afraid, Mary, for you have found favor with God. And now, you will conceive in your womb and bear a son, and you will name him Jesus. He will be great, and will be called the Son of the Most High, and the Lord God will give to him the throne of his ancestor David. He will reign over the house of Jacob forever, and of his kingdom there will be no end."

- Mary might well have felt afraid as she became aware of the presence of God. I spend this time in the presence of the same God and give thanks for the welcome and reassurance that God gives me. I ask Mary to be with me, to help me open my heart to God as she did.

14

- Mary said "Yes" to the plan that was outlined in the great sweep of the angel's words. I sometimes quail at the day-to-day challenges that I face. I ask God's help to remember that I can make God's ways evident even in small and ordinary ways.

The Second Week of Advent
## december 9–15

---

Something to think and pray about each day this week:

### The God Who Knows

In everything to do with prayer, we have our best model in Jesus himself. It is he who tells us both to ask for what we need, and that the Father knows our needs before we ask (Mt 6:9, 7:7). Whether we are praying for good weather for the wedding or pleading for the life of a sick friend, our prayers don't express something unknown to God. They don't bridge a gap between us and a God who is distant. God already knows. God is already with us in our desires. Our prayers are not like "making a wish" in the direction of God. All prayer involves some reaching out with childlike trust, even when the inner tone is chaotic or full of confusion. Prayer is always more than petition, even if petition is always a strand in prayer. Even if you do not use his words, all praying echoes the surrender of Jesus: not my will, but yours. We ask for what we think is best, but we try to hand everything over to the One who knows even better.

## The Presence of God
God is with me, but more,
God is within me, giving me existence.
Let me dwell for a moment on God's life-
giving presence
in my body, my mind, my heart
and in the whole of my life.

## Freedom
God is not foreign to my freedom.
Instead the Spirit breathes life into my most intimate desires,
gently nudging me towards all that is good.
I ask for the grace to let myself be enfolded by the Spirit.

**Consciousness**

Help me, Lord, to be more conscious of your
presence.
Teach me to recognize your presence in others.
Fill my heart with gratitude for the times your
love
has been shown to me through the care of
others.

**The Word**

I read the Word of God slowly, a few times
over, and I listen to what God is saying to me.
(Please turn to your scripture on the following
pages. Inspiration points are there should you
need them. When you are ready, return here to
continue.)

**Conversation**

How has God's Word moved me? Has it left
me cold?
Has it consoled me or moved me to act in a
new way?
I imagine Jesus standing or sitting beside me,
I turn and share my feelings with him.

## Conclusion

Glory be to the Father, and to the Son, and to the Holy Spirit,
As it was in the beginning, is now and ever shall be,
World without end. Amen.

### Sunday 9th December,
### Second Sunday of Advent          Mark 1:4–6

John the baptizer appeared in the wilderness, proclaiming a baptism of repentance for the forgiveness of sins. And people from the whole Judean countryside and all the people of Jerusalem were going out to him, and were baptized by him in the river Jordan, confessing their sins. Now John was clothed with camel's hair, with a leather belt around his waist, and he ate locusts and wild honey.

- John the Baptist preached forgiveness. This is one of the special gifts of God, and one of the big celebrations of Advent. We are a forgiven people, and we welcome the forgiveness of God in our repentance.

- This means we are firstly grateful for forgiveness— that we do not have to carry forever the burden of our sin, meanness, faults, and failings. God covers them over in mercy.

- The second step of welcoming forgiveness is to try to do better in life—to move on from this sinfulness and meanness to a life of care, compassion, love, and joy, and to make steps to forgive others.

### Monday 10th December          Luke 5:17–20

One day, while he was teaching, Pharisees and teachers of the law were sitting near by (they had come from every village of Galilee and Judea and from Jerusalem); and the power of the Lord was with him to heal. Just then some men came, carrying a paralyzed man on a bed. They were trying to bring him in and lay him before Jesus; but finding no way to bring him in because of the crowd, they went up on the roof and let him down with his bed through the tiles into the middle of the crowd in front of Jesus. When he saw their faith, he said, "Friend, your sins are forgiven you."

* When I come to pray, I do not come alone. I bring before Jesus all those people whose needs I know, all those for whom I have hopes. I lay them before Jesus so that they may receive the help and healing they need.

- Jesus speaks forgiveness to me. I receive the healing that he offers and ask to understand the new life Jesus seeks for me.

### Tuesday 11th December    Matthew 18:12–14

Jesus said to his disciples: "What do you think? If a shepherd has a hundred sheep, and one of them has gone astray, does he not leave the ninety-nine on the mountains and go in search of the one that went astray? And if he finds it, truly I tell you, he rejoices over it more than over the ninety-nine that never went astray. So it is not the will of your Father in heaven that one of these little ones should be lost."

- Jesus is the shepherd whose heart goes after the one who is lost. When I feel forlorn or lost, I have a special place in Jesus' heart. I allow myself to feel vulnerable, to be cherished, sought and found.

- I may sometimes want to have everything squared away and in order. It may be that I want to rely more on myself than on Jesus. Being in need is not demeaning when I am closer to the heart of Jesus.

### Wednesday 12th December    Matthew 11:28–30

Jesus said, "Come to me, all you that are weary and are carrying heavy burdens, and I will give you rest. Take my yoke upon you, and learn from me; for I am gentle and humble in heart, and you will find rest for your souls. For my yoke is easy, and my burden is light."

- The scribes and Pharisees laid heavy burdens on people by imposing on them the so-called "traditions of the elders," rules and regulations not found in the Jewish Scriptures. Jesus scorned these "traditions."

- Instead he urged his followers to take his "yoke," to accept his direction. Jesus' yoke is easy because what he teaches, no matter how challenging, gives meaning, direction, and peace of soul to a person's life.

**Thursday 13th December    Isaiah 41:17–20**

When the poor and needy seek water, and there is none, and their tongue is parched with thirst, I the LORD will answer them, I the God of Israel will not forsake them. I will open rivers on the bare heights, and fountains in the midst of the valleys; I will make the wilderness a pool of water, and the dry land springs of water. I will put in the wilderness the cedar, the acacia, the myrtle, and the olive; I will set in the desert the cypress, the plane and the pine together, so that all may see and know, all may consider and understand, that the hand of the LORD has done this, the Holy One of Israel has created it.

- Let's imagine the dramatic scene Isaiah paints: a desert, barren, parched, and lifeless where God's people starve and thirst. By God's gift we follow its transformation.

- Where is my world barren or loveless? Where do I see people thirsting for life?

- Can I bring this situation to the Lord?

### Friday 14th December   Matthew 11:16–19

Jesus spoke to the crowds, "But to what will I compare this generation? It is like children sitting in the marketplaces and calling to one another, 'We played the flute for you, and you did not dance; we wailed, and you did not mourn.' For John came neither eating nor drinking, and they say, 'He has a demon'; the Son of Man came eating and drinking, and they say, 'Look, a glutton and a drunkard, a friend of tax collectors and sinners!' Yet wisdom is vindicated by her deeds."

- The children playing in the marketplace might have seemed a trivial distraction to many, but to Jesus they offered an image of life. Perhaps I can take time to notice the small things in my life—the incidental happenings—and listen to what God may be saying to me in them.

- Jesus knew that he could not please all of the people around him. He remained true to his vision and truth. I pray that I may not become distracted from following Jesus by trying to win the approval of others.

**Saturday 15th December   Matthew 17:10–13**

And the disciples asked him, "Why, then, do the scribes say that Elijah must come first?" He replied, "Elijah is indeed coming and will restore all things; but I tell you that Elijah has already come, and they did not recognize him, but they did to him whatever they pleased. So also the Son of Man is about to suffer at their hands." Then the disciples understood that he was speaking to them about John the Baptist.

- The disciples brought their questions to Jesus, to hear what he might have to say. I bring the things that make me wonder, that raise questions for me, and lay them before Jesus in prayer. I listen carefully for his word.

- Neither John the Baptist nor Jesus was always recognized. I pray for the humility I need to act as Jesus did.

# december 16–22

Something to think and pray about each day this week:

## The Deepest Thirst

Follow the story in John's Gospel of Jesus' encounter at the well of Jacob. Imagine yourself the Samaritan woman. I come to the well on a simple errand, to fetch water for the house. To my surprise, a stranger accosts me and asks for a favor. He is a foreigner, the sort of man I would expect to be hostile. I try to work out what he is up to. Soon my need for water is forgotten. He explores my history. He knows me better than my closest friends. He speaks of a thirst that is deeper than my everyday appetite. He opens a vision of a world beyond our present divisions. I cannot keep this to myself. It is too important, too life-enhancing not to talk about. I go home and spread the news: "Come, see a

man who told me all that I ever did. Can this
be the Christ?"

## The Presence of God

What is present to me is what has a hold on
my becoming.
I reflect on the presence of God always there in
love,
amidst the many things that have a hold on
me.
I pause and pray that I may let God
affect my becoming in this precise moment.

## Freedom

There are very few people
who realize what God would make of them
if they abandoned themselves into his hands,
and let themselves be formed by his grace.
(St. Ignatius)
I ask for the grace to trust myself totally to
God's love.

**Consciousness**

In the presence of my loving Creator,
I look honestly at my feelings over the last day,
the highs, the lows, and the level ground.
Can I see where the Lord has been present?

**The Word**

God speaks to each one of us individually. I need
to listen to hear what he is saying to me. Read
the text a few times, then listen. (Please turn
to your scripture on the following pages. Inspiration points are there should you need them.
When you are ready, return here to continue.)

**Conversation**

What is stirring in me as I pray?
Am I consoled, troubled, left cold?
I imagine Jesus himself standing or sitting at
my side,
and share my feelings with him.

## Conclusion

Glory be to the Father, and to the Son, and to the Holy Spirit,
As it was in the beginning, is now and ever shall be,
World without end. Amen.

### Sunday 16th December,
### Third Sunday of Advent     John 1:6–8, 19–28

There was a man sent from God, whose name was John. He came as a witness to testify to the light, so that all might believe through him. He himself was not the light, but he came to testify to the light. This is the testimony given by John when the Jews sent priests and Levites from Jerusalem to ask him, "Who are you?" He confessed and did not deny it, but confessed, "I am not the Messiah." And they asked him, "What then? Are you Elijah?" He said, "I am not." "Are you the prophet?" He answered, "No." Then they said to him, "Who are you? Let us have an answer for those who sent us. What do you say about yourself?" He said, "I am the voice of one crying out in the wilderness, 'Make straight the way of the Lord,'" as the prophet Isaiah said. Now they had been sent from the Pharisees. They asked him, "Why then are you baptizing if you are neither the Messiah, nor Elijah, nor the prophet?" John answered

them, "I baptize with water. Among you stands one whom you do not know, the one who is coming after me; I am not worthy to untie the thong of his sandal." This took place in Bethany across the Jordan where John was baptizing.

- We are in the atmosphere of something about to happen. John the Baptist is still on the scene, pointing where to look, where to wait, how to expect the one who is to come. We get so used to Christmas and the coming of Christ that we hardly have any sense of expectation.

- Christmas is not meant to be quiet. It's meant to draw out many responses in us. This could be a week of active expectancy—to do something to prepare well for the Lord.

- How will you prepare for Christmas? Can you do something for the poor each day? Thank somebody genuinely each day for their place in your life? Say you are sorry to someone you hurt or forgive someone who hurt you?

### Monday 17th December     Matthew 1:1–7

An account of the genealogy of Jesus the Messiah, the son of David, the son of Abraham. Abraham was the father of Isaac, and Isaac the father of Jacob, and Jacob the father of Judah and his brothers, and Judah the father of Perez and Zerah by Tamar, and Perez the father of Hezron, and Hezron the father of Aram, and Aram the father of Aminadab, and Aminadab the father of Nahshon, and Nahshon the father of Salmon, and Salmon the father of Boaz by Rahab, and Boaz the father of Obed by Ruth, and Obed the father of Jesse, and Jesse the father of King David. And David was the father of Solomon by the wife of Uriah, and Solomon the father of Rehoboam. . . .

- This litany of names deserves to be read reverently, as all names do. I think of the lists that can easily dehumanize and pray that the dignity and experience of each person be respected. I consider that a life's story lies behind each name that I see today.

- I think of how my life and faith depend on so many others about whom I know so little. I pray for them with thanks.

## Tuesday 18th December   Matthew 1:18–24

Now the birth of Jesus the Messiah took place in this way. When his mother Mary had been engaged to Joseph, but before they lived together, she was found to be with child from the Holy Spirit. Her husband Joseph, being a righteous man and unwilling to expose her to public disgrace, planned to dismiss her quietly. But just when he had resolved to do this, an angel of the Lord appeared to him in a dream and said, "Joseph, son of David, do not be afraid to take Mary as your wife, for the child conceived in her is from the Holy Spirit. She will bear a son, and you are to name him Jesus, for he will save his people from their sins." All this took place to fulfill what had been spoken by the Lord through the prophet: "Look, the virgin shall conceive and bear a son, and they shall name him Emmanuel," which means, "God is

with us." When Joseph awoke from sleep, he did as the angel of the Lord commanded him; he took her as his wife.

- When God breaks in to human affairs it causes surprises and not a little initial upset.

- What must Joseph's first reaction have been? How could he have known what mysteries were afoot? Can I follow in imagination the steps he must have gone through before humbly accommodating himself to God's plans?

- What does this reality of God's "breaking in" say to my life and experience?

### Wednesday 19th December    Luke 1:5–25

In the days of King Herod of Judea, there was a priest named Zechariah, who belonged to the priestly order of Abijah. His wife was a descendant of Aaron, and her name was Elizabeth. Both of them were righteous before God, living blamelessly according to all the commandments and regulations of the Lord. But they had no children, because Elizabeth was barren, and

both were getting on in years. Once when he was serving as priest before God and his section was on duty, he was chosen by lot, according to the custom of the priesthood, to enter the sanctuary of the Lord and offer incense. Now at the time of the incense offering, the whole assembly of the people was praying outside. Then there appeared to him an angel of the Lord, standing at the right side of the altar of incense. When Zechariah saw him, he was terrified; and fear overwhelmed him. But the angel said to him, "Do not be afraid, Zechariah, for your prayer has been heard. Your wife Elizabeth will bear you a son, and you will name him John. You will have joy and gladness, and many will rejoice at his birth, for he will be great in the sight of the Lord. He must never drink wine or strong drink; even before his birth he will be filled with the Holy Spirit. He will turn many of the people of Israel to the Lord their God. With the spirit and power of Elijah he will go before him, to turn the hearts of parents to their children, and the disobedient to the wisdom of the righteous, to make ready a people prepared for the Lord." Zechariah said to the angel, "How will I know that this is so? For I am an old man, and my wife is getting on in years." The angel replied, "I am Gabriel. I stand in the presence of God, and I have been sent to speak to you and to bring you this good news. But now, because you did not believe my words, which will be fulfilled in their time, you will become mute, unable to speak, until the day these things occur." Meanwhile the people were waiting for Zechariah, and wondered at his delay in the sanctuary. When he did come out, he could not speak to them, and they realized that he had seen a vision in the sanctuary. He kept motioning to them and remained unable to speak. When his time of service was ended, he went to his home. After those days his wife Elizabeth conceived, and for five months she remained in seclusion. She said, "This is what the Lord has done for me when he looked favorably on me and took away the disgrace I have endured among my people."

- Zechariah served as a priest in the Jerusalem Temple. One of the duties of the priests was to keep the brazier burning that stood on the altar of incense in front of the Holy of Holies. They would fill the brazier with fresh incense before the morning sacrifice, and again at the evening sacrifice.

- It was during such an occasion that God's messenger, Gabriel, appears and foretells the birth of John the Baptist. Later, when his wife Elizabeth, against all odds, finds herself pregnant, she proclaims, "This is what the Lord has done for me when he looked favorably on me and took away the disgrace I have endured among my people." Barrenness was considered a humiliation, and even a punishment from God.

- As I contemplate this scene, am I ever awed by the great things God has done for me during my life?

**Thursday 20th December**     Luke 1:38

Then Mary said, "Here am I, the servant of the Lord; let it be with me according to your word." Then the angel departed from her.

- Mary's "Here am I" has such direct simplicity that it reminds me that I am often distracted. I consider how too much looking ahead or back distracts me from being present to myself—where God wants to meet me.

- "The angel departed." Mary did not live in the glow of the angel's presence but took the message of God's presence into her daily life. I value this time of quiet and ask that it nourish me in the busy moments of my life.

**Friday 21st December**     Luke 1:39–45

In those days Mary set out and went with haste to a Judean town in the hill country, where she entered the house of Zechariah and greeted Elizabeth. When Elizabeth heard Mary's greeting, the child leaped in her womb. And Elizabeth was filled with the Holy Spirit and exclaimed with a loud cry, "Blessed are you among women, and blessed is the fruit of your womb. And why has this happened to me, that the mother of my Lord comes to me? For as soon as I heard the sound of your greeting, the child in my womb leaped for joy. And blessed is she who believed that there would be a fulfillment of what was spoken to her by the Lord."

- The Spirit of God in Elizabeth rejoiced in the presence of Mary. I pray for those who have been friends to me, for all whose companionship or example lifts my heart.

- An expectant mother, Mary set out on her journey. She carried the Word within her. I draw inspiration from this scene and see in it a reminder of who I am this day: I carry the Word of God in me as nourishment for me and for those around me.

### Saturday 22nd December    Luke 1:46–56

And Mary said, "My soul magnifies the Lord, and my spirit rejoices in God my Savior, for he has looked with favor on the lowliness of his servant. Surely, from now on all generations will call me blessed; for the Mighty One has done great things for me, and holy is his name. His mercy is for those who fear him from generation to generation. He has shown strength with his arm; he has scattered the proud in the thoughts of their hearts. He has brought down the powerful from their thrones, and lifted up the lowly; he has filled the hungry with good things, and sent the rich away empty. He has helped his servant Israel, in remembrance of his mercy, according to the promise he made to our ancestors, to Abraham and to his descendants forever." And Mary remained with Elizabeth about three months and then returned to her home.

- With Mary, I count my blessings, not as a matter of pride or achievement, but to recognize where God is at work in my life.

The Fourth Week of Advent/Christmas
## december 23–29

---

Something to think and pray about each day this week:

**Meditating on Advent**

Now more than at any other time we need to insulate ourselves from the constant pressure from advertisers and media, telling us what to buy and how to spend at Christmas. Come back to some simple reminder of the meaning of the feast, like Alice Meynell's *Advent Meditation*:

> No sudden thing of glory and fear
> Was the Lord's coming; but the dear
> Slow Nature's days followed each other
> To form the Saviour from His Mother
> —One of the children of the year.

## The Presence of God

God is with me, but more, God is within me.
Let me dwell for a moment on God's life-
giving presence
in my body, in my mind, in my heart,
as I sit here, right now.

## Freedom

A thick and shapeless tree-trunk would never
believe
that it could become a statue, admired as a
miracle of sculpture,
and would never submit itself to the chisel of
the sculptor,
who sees by her genius what she can make of
it. (St. Ignatius)
I ask for the grace to let myself be shaped by
my loving Creator.

## Consciousness

Knowing that God loves me unconditionally,
I can afford to be honest about how I am.
How has the last day been, and how do I feel
now?
I share my feelings openly with the Lord.

**The Word**

I read the Word of God slowly, a few times
over, and I listen to what God is saying to me.
(Please turn to your scripture on the following
pages. Inspiration points are there should you
need them. When you are ready, return here to
continue.)

**Conversation**

Do I notice myself reacting as I pray with the
Word of God?
Do I feel challenged, comforted, angry?
Imagining Jesus sitting or standing by me,
I speak out my feelings, as one trusted friend
to another.

**Conclusion**

Glory be to the Father, and to the Son, and to
the Holy Spirit,
As it was in the beginning, is now and ever
shall be,
World without end. Amen.

### Sunday 23rd December,
### Fourth Sunday of Advent    Luke 1:26–38

In the sixth month the angel Gabriel was sent by God to a town in Galilee called Nazareth, to a virgin engaged to a man whose name was Joseph, of the house at David. The virgin's name was Mary. And he came to her and said, "Greetings, favored one! The Lord is with you." But she was much perplexed by his words and pondered what sort of greeting this might be. The angel said to her, "Do not be afraid, Mary, for you have found favor with God. And now, you will conceive in your womb and bear a son, and you will name him Jesus. He will be great, and will be called the Son of the Most High, and the Lord God will give to him the throne of his ancestor David. He will reign over the house of Jacob forever, and of his kingdom there will be no end." Mary said to the angel, "How can this be, since I am a virgin?" The angel said to her, "The Holy Spirit will come upon you, and the power of the Most High will overshadow you;

therefore the child to be born will be holy; he will be called Son of God. And now, your relative Elizabeth in her old age has also conceived a son; and this is the sixth month for her who was said to be barren. For nothing will be impossible with God." Then Mary said, "Here am I, the servant of the Lord; let it be with me according to your word." Then the angel departed from her.

- Christmas highlights the belief that God is in all of us. We can ignore that, or we can help God be found in all of us. God is active through each of us for each other.

- In the visit of Mary, God came close to Elizabeth in the ordinary and homely moments of every day. These Advent and Christmas days give us the space to allow the huge eternal mystery to become part of the everyday.

- Pride and humility are in the picture as Mary prays her *Magnificat*. Mary rejoices in being a blessed, lowly servant. I think of how this description relates to how I am now.

### Monday 24th December         Luke 1:67–79

Then his father Zechariah was filled with the Holy Spirit and spoke this prophecy: "Blessed be the Lord God of Israel, for he has looked favorably on his people and redeemed them. He has raised up a mighty savior for us in the house of his servant David, as he spoke through the mouth of his holy prophets from of old, that we would be saved from our enemies and from the hand of all who hate us. Thus he has shown the mercy promised to our ancestors, and has remembered his holy covenant, the oath that he swore to our ancestor Abraham, to grant us that we, being rescued from the hands of our enemies, might serve him without fear, in holiness and righteousness before him all our days. And you, child, will be called the prophet of the Most High; for you will go before the Lord to prepare his ways, to give knowledge of salvation to his people by the forgiveness of their sins. By the tender mercy of our God, the dawn from on high will break upon us, to give light to those

who sit in darkness and in the shadow of death,
to guide our feet into the way of peace."

- Every day, this prayer of Zechariah becomes the
  morning prayer of thousands of people across the
  world. I read it slowly, letting the words reveal
  their meaning for me today.

- Zechariah is profoundly aware of his heritage,
  seeing God's action in the past as having promise
  for the future. I draw encouragement from my
  own story, allowing God to bless me with hope
  and confidence in continued blessing.

### Tuesday 25th December,
### Feast of the Nativity of the Lord    John 1:1–5

In the beginning was the Word, and the Word
was with God, and the Word was God. He
was in the beginning with God. All things came
into being through him, and without him not
one thing came into being. What has come into
being in him was life, and the life was the light
of all people. The light shines in the darkness,
and the darkness did not overcome it.

No love that in a family dwells,
No caroling in frosty air,
Nor all the steeple-shaking bells
Can with this single Truth compare —
That God was Man in Palestine
And lives today in Bread and Wine.
(G. K. Chesterton)

## Wednesday 26th December,
## St. Stephen, the first martyr   Matthew 10:17–22

Jesus said to his apostles, "Beware of them, for they will hand you over to councils and flog you in their synagogues; and you will be dragged before governors and kings because of me, as a testimony to them and the Gentiles. When they hand you over, do not worry about how you are to speak or what you are to say; for what you are to say will be given to you at that time; for it is not you who speak, but the Spirit of your Father speaking through you. Brother will betray brother to death, and a father his child, and children will rise against parents and have them put to death; and you will be hated by all because of my name. But the one who endures to the end will be saved."

- Immediately after remembering the birth of Jesus, the Church remembers the first martyr. Birth and death are intimately connected with Jesus. The word for the place he was born is the same as the word for the "upper room," where he had the last supper. We know that the destiny of this child is for a cruel death.

- The upper room was also the place for the coming of the Spirit. In all of life, birth, and death and all that is in-between is the blessing of the Spirit.

## Thursday 27th December, St. John, Evangelist          John 20:1a, 2–8

Early on the first day of the week, while it was still dark, Mary Magdalene came to the tomb and saw that the stone had been removed from the tomb. So she ran and went to Simon Peter and the other disciple, the one whom Jesus loved, and said to them, "They have taken the Lord out of the tomb, and we do not know where they have laid him." Then Peter and the other disciple set out and went toward the tomb. The two were running together, but the other disciple outran Peter and reached the tomb first. He bent down to look in and saw the linen wrappings lying there, but he did not go in. Then Simon Peter came, following him, and went into the tomb. He saw the linen wrappings lying there, and the cloth that had been on Jesus' head, not lying with the linen wrappings but rolled up in a place by itself. Then the other disciple, who reached the tomb first, also went in, and he saw and believed.

- It is sometimes tempting to cling to the glow of Christmas. While I value the gift of this season, this Easter scene reminds me that faith calls me to move on, to seek the Risen Lord.

- When Mary Magdalene did not find Jesus where she expected, she went first to her community. As questions arise for me, I bring them to God and to others whom I trust.

**Friday, 28th December,**
**The Holy Innocents**          Matthew 2:16–18

When Herod saw that he had been tricked by the wise men, he was infuriated, and he sent and killed all the children in and around Bethlehem who were two years old or under, according to the time that he had learned from the wise men. Then was fulfilled what had been spoken through the prophet Jeremiah: "A voice was heard in Ramah, wailing and loud lamentation, Rachel weeping for her children; she refused to be consoled, because they are no more."

- This terrible scene evokes the genocides and atrocities that still happen today.

- Herod's action was motivated by his pride and self-seeking. As I pray for all leaders, I ask God to heal me of any false image I have of myself. I pray with compassion for all who are affected by violence and cruelty.

**Saturday 29th December**     Luke 2:27–32

Guided by the Spirit, Simeon came into the temple; and when the parents brought in the child Jesus, to do for him what was customary under the law, Simeon took him in his arms and praised God, saying, "Master, now you are dismissing your servant in peace, according to your word; for my eyes have seen your salvation, which you have prepared in the presence of all peoples, a light for revelation to the Gentiles and for glory to your people Israel."

- Simeon's example is of patient hope, as he waited around the temple for a sign of God's salvation. I ask for a strengthening of my hope and faith as I wait on the Lord.

- Each day, thousands across the world make this their night prayer. Perhaps I might read it this evening, with acceptance and quiet joy, in gratitude for God's work through each one of us.

# december 30–january 6

Something to think and pray about each day this week:

## God Incarnate

A married woman once told a group of her friends: "When my husband looks at me, I am so much greater and richer than when I look at myself. I sense so much more potential in me." Her husband added: "When I experience my wife's loving gaze, I feel a sense of inner growth that seems to be lacking if I just look at myself in the mirror." We experience this in Jesus' birth. God looks at us through human eyes for the first time, and in that gaze we begin to know our value and preciousness. The Incarnation reveals to us our worth in the sight of God. He loves us enough to share this mortal flesh with us. In prayer I think how God is waiting for me, looking at me.

### The Presence of God

As I sit here, the beating of my heart,
the ebb and flow of my breathing, the move-
ments of my mind
are all signs of God's ongoing creation of me.
I pause for a moment, and become aware
of this presence of God within me.

### Freedom

I ask for the grace
to let go of my own concerns
and be open to what God is asking of me,
to let myself be guided and formed by my loving Creator.

### Consciousness

In the presence of my loving Creator,
I look honestly at my feelings over the last day,
the highs, the lows, and the level ground.
Can I see where the Lord has been present?

### The Word

I take my time to read the Word of God,
slowly, a few times, allowing myself to dwell

on anything that strikes me. (Please turn to
your scripture on the following pages. Inspiration points are there should you need them.
When you are ready, return here to continue.)

## Conversation

Remembering that I am still in God's presence,
I imagine Jesus himself standing or sitting
beside me,
and say whatever is on my mind, whatever is
in my heart,
speaking as one friend to another.

## Conclusion

Glory be to the Father, and to the Son, and to
the Holy Spirit,
As it was in the beginning, is now and ever
shall be,
World without end. Amen.

## Sunday 30th December,
## The Holy Family      Matthew 2:13–15

Now after they had left, an angel of the Lord appeared to Joseph in a dream and said, "Get up, take the child and his mother, and flee to Egypt, and remain there until I tell you; for Herod is about to search for the child, to destroy him." Then Joseph got up, took the child and his mother by night, and went to Egypt, and remained there until the death of Herod. This was to fulfill what had been spoken by the Lord through the prophet, "Out of Egypt I have called my son."

- Just after the wonders and signs of the visit of the Magi, Joseph is ready to move on. I pray that I may be able to relish inspiration wherever I find it, yet always remain poised to act.

- Joseph, Mary, and Jesus lived the lives of exiles. I pray for all who are away from home at this time because of political conditions and think of the exiles I encounter.

### Monday 31st December    John 1:16–18

From his fullness we have all received, grace upon grace. The law indeed was given through Moses; grace and truth came through Jesus Christ. No one has ever seen God. It is God the only Son, who is close to the Father's heart, who has made him known.

- This time of prayer is one way in which I receive the truth and grace that God wants to offer me. I prepare myself to receive blessings from the very heart of God.

- "Grace upon grace"; I picture an abundance of blessing, a cascade of goodness. This is what God desires for me. I ask that I not be content with less.

### Tuesday 1st January,
### Solemnity of Mary, Mother of God    Luke 2:16–21

So they went with haste and found Mary and Joseph, and the child lying in the manger. When they saw this, they made known what had been told them about this child; and all who heard it were amazed at what the shepherds told them. But Mary treasured all these words and pondered them in her heart. The shepherds returned, glorifying and praising God for all they had heard and seen, as it had been told them. After eight days had passed, it was time to circumcise the child; and he was called Jesus, the name given by the angel before he was conceived in the womb.

- God's messengers tell the shepherds something astonishing, that a baby boy lying in a manger is both Messiah and Lord, God and Saviour! They, in their turn, repeat the angels' extraordinary message to Mary and Joseph.

- As Jesus grew and developed, Mary must have pondered all these things as she laced his sandals, prepared his meals, soothed him when he cried, and watched over him as he learned how to use carpenter's tools. Like any mother, she must have pondered what the future had in store for her son. I too am called to ponder Jesus' life so that his ways of thinking and his value system may become mine.

**Wednesday 2nd January**          John 1:19–28

This is the testimony given by John when the Jews sent priests and Levites from Jerusalem to ask him, "Who are you?" He confessed and did not deny it, but confessed, "I am not the Messiah." And they asked him, "What then? Are you Elijah?" He said, "I am not." "Are you the prophet?" He answered, "No." Then they said to him, "Who are you? Let us have an answer for those who sent us. What do you say about yourself?" He said, "I am the voice of one crying out in the wilderness, 'Make straight the way of the Lord,'" as the prophet Isaiah said. Now they had been sent from the Pharisees. They asked him, "Why then are you baptizing if you are neither the Messiah, nor Elijah, nor the prophet?" John answered them, "I baptize with water. Among you stands one whom you do not know, the one who is coming after me; I am not worthy to untie the thong of his sandal." This took place in Bethany across the Jordan where John was baptizing.

- When asked who he is, John the Baptist replies that he is "the voice of one crying in the wilderness, 'Make straight the way of the Lord.'" John compares himself to an engineer shouting out orders as the royal road is being prepared for the arrival of the king, or, in this case, for Jesus.

- What preparations am I making so that I am ready to welcome Jesus into my heart today?

### Thursday 3rd January      John 1:29–34

The next day John saw Jesus coming toward him and declared, "Here is the Lamb of God who takes away the sin of the world! This is he of whom I said, 'After me comes a man who ranks ahead of me because he was before me.' I myself did not know him; but I came baptizing with water for this reason, that he might be revealed to Israel." And John testified, "I saw the Spirit descending from heaven like a dove, and it remained on him. I myself did not know him, but the one who sent me to baptize with water said to me, 'He on whom you see the Spirit descend and remain is the one who baptizes with the Holy Spirit.' And I myself have seen and have testified that this is the Son of God."

- Our prayer brings us in touch with the Son of God who walked our earth. We pray in the presence of the One who lives in the Heaven of God's presence, and is also close to each of us. His essential quality is firstly that he takes away the sin of the world.

- Prayer purifies us each day, forgives us and calls us into fuller friendship with the one who is Son of God and son of Mary, child of heaven and born of earth.

### Friday 4th January        John 1:35–39

The next day John again was standing with two of his disciples, and as he watched Jesus walk by, he exclaimed, "Look, here is the Lamb of God!" The two disciples heard him say this, and they followed Jesus. When Jesus turned and saw them following, he said to them, "What are you looking for?" They said to him, "Rabbi" (which translated means Teacher), "where are you staying?" He said to them, "Come and see."

They came and saw where he was staying, and they remained with him that day.

- Jesus asks all would-be followers to spend time with him. He asks them to "come and see." By contemplating and meditating on the Gospels, I come to know Jesus more intimately and more personally.

- The various disciples invited one another to "come and see" Jesus. Do I ever share my experience of knowing, loving, and serving Jesus with others?

### Saturday 5th January      John 1:43–51

The next day Jesus decided to go to Galilee. He found Philip and said to him, "Follow me." Now Philip was from Bethsaida, the city of Andrew and Peter. Philip found Nathanael and said to him, "We have found him about whom Moses in the law and also the prophets wrote, Jesus son of Joseph from Nazareth." Nathanael said to him, "Can anything good come out of Nazareth?" Philip said to him, "Come and see." When Jesus saw Nathanael coming toward him, he said of him, "Here is truly an Israelite in whom there is no deceit!" Nathanael asked him, "Where did you get to know me?" Jesus answered, "I saw you under the fig tree before Philip called you." Nathanael replied, "Rabbi, you are the Son of God! You are the King of Israel!" Jesus answered, "Do you believe because I told you that I saw you under the fig tree? You will see greater things than these." And he said to him, "Very truly, I tell you, you will see heaven opened and the angels of God ascending and descending upon the Son of Man."

- "Can anything good come out of Nazareth?" Nathaniel asks rather cynically. People are often judged by where they come from, by the way they speak, by their status in society. Do I do that?

**Sunday 6th January,**

**The Epiphany of the Lord**     Matthew 2:1–2, 7–12

In the time of King Herod, after Jesus was born in Bethlehem of Judea, wise men from the East came to Jerusalem, asking, "Where is the child who has been born king of the Jews? For we observed his star at its rising, and have come to pay him homage." Herod secretly called for the wise men and learned from them the exact time when the star had appeared. Then he sent them to Bethlehem, saying, "Go and search diligently for the child; and when you have found him, bring me word so that I may also go and pay him homage." When they had heard the king, they set out; and there, ahead of them, went the star that they had seen at its rising, until it stopped over the place where the child was. When they saw that the star had stopped, they were overwhelmed with joy. On entering the house, they saw the child with Mary his mother; and they knelt down and paid him homage. Then, opening their treasure chests, they offered him gifts of gold, frankincense, and myrrh. And having been warned in a dream not to return to Herod, they left for their own country by another road.

- Can you remember some time in life when you were overcome with joy?

- Joy is a gift from God and a share in the nature of God, for God is joy. Allow this joy to be part of your life and part of your prayer this day. Allow the tough times to find their place there, too.

## introduction to the advent retreat

---

We are moving into the season of Advent, and for most of us, this will mean that we are in "waiting" mode—but waiting for what? This retreat will help us to find out. We will find out what's going on between ourselves and God, and how we might move forward, even a little. So, welcome!

Believe that you are being given a special invitation by God to give this time to meet him. You meet God in the deepest dimension of your heart. There you are at your truest and best self. Ask for the gift of a silent heart to be able to hear God's whisper there. Then you will catch on to what God wishes for you this Christmastide.

A retreat is an inner journey, but where it may lead is as yet unknown. You may well be surprised or encouraged, challenged, or excited at what happens. You may become puzzled or fearful: Perhaps God may be hinting that your

life should take a new direction—think of Our
Lady at the Annunciation. By staying with the
prayer with an open mind and a generous heart,
the results will bring you peace. God is a God
of consolation and waits to be gracious to you
(2 Cor 1:3; Is 30:18).

**Outline of the Retreat**

The retreat is organized into four sessions.
You can complete them in a single day or spread
them out over the four weeks of Advent, or take
them in some other way. Just go gently, at your
own pace. There are advantages in going slowly
and staying a while with each Gospel character
you meet.

As you start out, have in mind a simple image
of the stable in Bethlehem with its central characters and animals. In each of the four periods
of the retreat, I will bring different characters
center stage and ask them to befriend you as
you seek the Christ Child. Make them your
"patrons" and pray for their help. They will back

you up, and so you will not feel alone and lost in your prayer time.

Events or conversations may provide important material for your prayer. For example, as I prepared an Advent weekend last year for a group, I was struck over and over again by the number of references to angels. They seemed to crop up all over the place in the Christmas story and played quite a part in the different scenes. Because of this, I began to think that angels might be able to do something for me! This changed my own approach to Advent. Perhaps you might ask your angel to keep a special watch over you as you travel through your retreat!

## Preparation for Each Prayer Session

Work out in advance a set of suitable prayer times. Decide how long you are going to give yourself for each session. Rhythms help us to settle down, and to anticipate what is ahead. Try to be generous: God rewards generous hearts. Half an hour may be suitable. St. Ignatius also suggests that whatever time you allocate to your prayer, you should be faithful to it, even if you are bored or find it difficult, distracting, dry or feel you are getting nowhere. In prayer we offer God goodwill, time and space. God does the rest.

Next choose a suitable place where you are likely to be undisturbed: put your phone on silent! Take up your preferred prayer posture—kneeling, sitting, or lying down.

**Breathing Exercise**

A breathing exercise can help to slow you down, relax you and focus you. There are many breathing exercises, but only one can be given here. If it helps, good. If not, try another. We learn only by experience what helps us.

Settle yourself. Begin to quietly breathe in and out through your nostrils. Imagine the room you are in as being filled with a coloured air. As you draw the air deep into your body through your nostrils you can visualise—in your imagination—that same coloured air making its way down from your nostrils through your throat and chest. Now, as if you had a glass body, you can see it making its way from your shoulders down your arms and working its way to your fingers. Also note the air as it travels downwards through your chest area right down to the pit of your stomach. Keep the quite, gentle breathing pattern working for you as it brings you into a relaxed state.

## Beginning the Prayer

Imagine God looking at you. How does God look at you? Has God a bored or angry or loving look? To accept the divine invitation to move forward into the unknown, you need to be aware of God's infinite and unconditional love for you. Think of the phrase with which a French mystic summed up her relationship with God: *"You gazed on me—and you smiled!"* Allow God to smile at you, and allow yourself to smile back! Perhaps much of the prayer time is spent here, but that will be fine!

Now ask God for what you need. Perhaps ask in this Advent time *"to see him more clearly, love him more dearly, and follow him more nearly."*

Slowly read the Scripture passage for the particular session, as if it were a coded message for you to decipher and then find a treasure. During the rest of the day you may find yourself coming back to particular phrases rich and meaningful for you.

Try to form a moving picture of the scene in your imagination. Let the scene unfold, and get into it, rather than remain an outsider. Prayer is not a spectator event! Ask the characters if you can join in with them. The Scripture passages for each of the four sessions are given below. Use the steps offered above (so far as they help you) each time you prepare to pray. Use the meditation points given after the Gospel passages (so far as they help you) to stay in touch with the mystery that is before you. Chat with the persons in the scene "as one friend chats to another" (St. Ignatius).

**Reviewing your Prayer**

It is often easier, St. Ignatius suggests, to see things more clearly in retrospect than when they are going on. Jotting down a few notes—as you might do if you keep track of your dreams—will help you clarify what otherwise is quickly forgotten. After each prayer session you can ask yourself what went on for you.

- What did I experience during the prayer time?

- Does anything jump out that was especially attractive or appealing to me or did something cause me disquiet? What might this mean?

- Might it be possible that God is asking anything special of me?

- Did I do what I could to stay focused in the time of prayer?

- Prayer is a relationship between God and myself: it is an "I and You" affair! So did I talk with God and the characters I met, or simply think about them?

Session One

# our lady and the angel
## (Lk 1:26–38)

*I read the story as if I have never read it before:*

In the sixth month the angel Gabriel was sent by God to a town in Galilee called Nazareth, to a virgin engaged to a man whose name was Joseph, of the house of David. The virgin's name was Mary. And he came to her and said, "Greetings, favoured one! The Lord is with you." But she was much perplexed by his words and pondered what sort of greeting this might be. The angel said to her, "Do not be afraid, Mary, for you have found favour with God. And now, you will conceive in your womb and bear a son, and you will name him Jesus. He will be great, and will be called the Son of the Most High, and the Lord God will give to him the throne of his ancestor David. He will reign over the house of Jacob for ever, and of his kingdom there will be no end." Mary said to the angel, "How can this be, since I am a virgin?" The angel said to her, "The Holy Spirit will come upon you, and the power of the Most High will overshadow you; therefore the child to be born will be holy; he will be called Son of God. And now, your relative Elizabeth in her old age has also conceived a son; and this is the sixth month for her who was said to be barren. For nothing will be impossible with God." Then Mary said, "Here am I, the servant of the Lord; let it be with me according to your word." Then the angel departed from her.

### In the silence I set the scene:

- First I imagine Nazareth and Mary's home.

- Next I think about Mary: What is she like? She is so unimportant: young, unmarried, childless, female, poor, living in the back of beyond! What goes on in her mind?

- Imagine the angel Gabriel coming. What day is it, and what time? Think of the first moments of their meeting.

- The angel was clear about the task s/he had to do. I talk with the angel: "Who gave you that task? Why? Why choose this girl?"

- I talk with Mary: "How much did you understand when the angel spoke? What made you say 'yes' at this life-changing moment?"

- I say to her: "You were so open and trusting!" How does she respond?

- I contemplate her with admiration: She seems so open to all possibilities. She does not insist on controlling her future. She trusts in God's goodness to carry her through all difficulties.

### Now I think about my own life:

- How would I have been if the angel had visited me?

- What proposal might the angel have had for me?

- Have I, in fact, ever been visited by a messenger of God, someone who was trying to help me to realize what God wanted me to do? If so, when might that have been? Where? Why?

- How did I respond? Did I respond at all?

- Do I control my life as if it were mine alone and not given me by God?

I chat with God, with Gabriel, and with Mary as my heart suggests. I finish with a prayer to my guardian angel asking for protection during this retreat. Finally, I review my prayer.

the wise men search for jesus
(Mt 2:1–8)

*I read the story aloud, as if I have never read it before.*

In the time of King Herod, after Jesus was born in Bethlehem of Judea, wise men from the East came to Jerusalem, asking, "Where is the child who has been born king of the Jews? For we observed his star at its rising, and have come to pay him homage." When King Herod heard this, he was frightened, and all Jerusalem with him; and calling together all the chief priests and scribes of the people, he inquired of them where the Messiah was to be born. They told him, "In Bethlehem of Judea; for so it has been written by the prophet:

"And you, Bethlehem, in the land of
Judah, are by no means least among
the rulers of Judah;
for from you shall come a ruler
who is to shepherd my people Israel."

Then Herod secretly called for the wise men
and learned from them the exact time when
the star had appeared. Then he sent them to
Bethlehem, saying, "Go and search diligently
for the child; and when you have found him,
bring me word so that I may also go and pay
him homage."

### In the silence, I enter into the scene:

- I use my imagination to paint the event or recreate the story in my head.

- Do I want to go with the wise men? Do they accept me as a companion? Am I able for the trek? I chat with them: Perhaps I can be their camel herd, their cook, or their scribe.

- I visualize them deliberating about the wisdom of setting out. What has prompted them to make this journey? Do people laugh and jeer at our party as it moves off?

- I can discern that they are searching for something. They have only a star to guide them. I identify with them.

- What hindrances do we encounter together as we wander along?

- As I make my way along with them, note the mood and feelings of each of them. I let each of them chat with you in turn. I tell one of them my story and he listens well.

### *Now I think about my own life:*

- Do I see my life thus far as a journey? Where did it begin, what were its stages, where am I now?

- What—or Who—has been guiding me all along the way?

- Can I imagine God admiring many of the wise decisions I made?

- Has God unobtrusively intervened to save me from the consequences of some of my unwise decisions?

- Am I prepared to go out of my way to find where the Christ child might be for me this Christmas?

- Am I learning anything about myself as I journey with them in my imagination? I might ask them for some of their wisdom and for the ability to have eyes to see, ears to hear what God may suggest to me.

- During the day, I can ask the wise men to be my companions. You might be helped to get into their mindset by reading T. S. Eliot's wonderful poem, *The Journey of the Magi.*

- What obstacles am I meeting up with as I try to obtain more self-knowledge through this prayer exercise? Am I resisting new thoughts or insights? Have I a generous heart?

I chat with God and with the wise men as my heart suggests. I finish with a prayer of thanksgiving to God for all those who have been like shining stars for me over my lifetime. I thank God too that I have been a star for many others. I call to mind some of these people and bless them. Finally, I review my prayer as in the above. St. Ignatius of Loyola talks about repetition in prayer. It can be helpful to go over a prayer exercise again: we pluck low-hanging fruit first, but there can be other fruit on the upper branches!

# the wise men find jesus
### (Mt 2:9–12)

_____

*After preparation, I read the story as if I had
never read it before, or perhaps imagine Mary
whispering it to me. I listen with wonder, as
when I first heard it.*

When they had heard the king, they set out;
and there, ahead of them, went the star
that they had seen at its rising, until it stopped
over the place where the child was. When they
saw that the star had stopped, they were overwhelmed with joy. On entering the house, they
saw the child with Mary his mother; and they
knelt down and paid him homage. Then, opening their treasure chests, they offered him gifts
of gold, frankincense, and myrrh. And having
been warned in a dream not to return to Herod,
they left for their own country by another road.

### *In the silence, I enter into the scene:*

- I travel with the wise men, remembering that the rewards of the journey were uncertain and its risks great. Yet still they started out. What faith! What courage!

- They survived by hope. They had no human certainties or structures to support them.

- The wise men did not only have to contend with natural hazards along their route. There were those who wished to actively frustrate them from achieving their goal. For a moment, I stay with the figure of Herod. What was he like?

- I follow the wise men in my imagination as they trudge along carrying their gifts for a king whom they knew so little about. They wanted to give of their best.

- What was it like for them to find the house with Jesus there? Did they cry a bit? Despite being exhausted, do they brighten up, knowing that the long journey was infinitely worthwhile? I ask questions, I listen well.

### *Now I think about my own life:*

- I think for a moment about my own gifts and my generosity of spirit. What are those gifts? How much do I want to offer them to Christ?

- Are there people or situations that are actively hindering me in my faith journey? If so, who/what are they? What can I do about them?

- What am I learning about the sort of person God is?

- I am always being drawn onward to a deeper life with God. Am I happy to be led or do I resist changes?

I chat with Mary, Joseph, and the wise men as my heart suggests. I give thanks to God for the wise people in my life, and ask that in turn I may be a helpful and welcoming presence to those I meet on my life's journey. Finally, I review my prayer. What gave me joy and consolation? The touch of God was there, so I treasure it.

# the shepherds and the angels
### (Lk 2:6–20)

*After the moments of preparation, read the
Christmas story as if you had never read it before,
or perhaps imagine Joseph telling it to you. You
listen with the wonder of a child.*

While they were there, the time came for
her to deliver her child. And she gave
birth to her firstborn son and wrapped him
in bands of cloth, and laid him in a manger,
because there was no place for them in the inn.
In that region there were shepherds living in the
fields, keeping watch over their flock by night.
Then an angel of the Lord stood before them,
and the glory of the Lord shone around them,
and they were terrified. But the angel said to
them, "Do not be afraid; for see—I am bringing
you good news of great joy for all the people:
to you is born this day in the city of David a
Saviour, who is the Messiah, the Lord. This will

be a sign for you: you will find a child wrapped in bands of cloth and lying in a manger." And suddenly there was with the angel a multitude of the heavenly host, praising God and saying,

"Glory to God in the highest heaven,
and on earth peace among those whom
he favours!"

When the angels had left them and gone into heaven, the shepherds said to one another, "Let us go now to Bethlehem and see this thing that has taken place, which the Lord has made known to us." So they went with haste and found Mary and Joseph, and the child lying in the manger. When they saw this, they made known what had been told them about this child; and all who heard it were amazed at what the shepherds told them. But Mary treasured all these words and pondered them in her heart. The shepherds returned, glorifying and praising God for all they had heard and seen, as it had been told them.

### *In the silence, I enter into the scene:*

- By now I can perhaps work through the scene on my own. What I work out for myself is more valuable than what others offer, because prayer is all about that personal and unique relationship which God has with me. After the retreat, I will be able to take up any Gospel scene, enter into it, and meet God there.

- I imagine that I am with Joseph in the cave at Bethlehem. This animal shelter is too simple for the sophisticated to bother much with. But its message is rich for the poor and the broken. Jesus wants to be born into human hearts now, just as they are at this moment, in all their brokenness, pain, and emptiness. I see the empty manger before Jesus is placed in it. He wasn't looking for the perfect place then. He's not looking for it now.

- I let Mary tell me her story in her own words. I watch her face as she speaks.

- I go with the shepherds now in my imagination as they hurry off to the stable. Why were they chosen to celebrate the first Christmas party?

- The sight that greets them is simple yet profound. God has visited His people. There isn't another God of a different sort, somewhere in heaven, more fearsome and awesome than this child. This Child is God—incarnate! This is divine Love—incarnate! This is what God is like. And it is all done *for me*.

- First I notice the infant figure of Jesus as he lies there. How helpless and vulnerable he is. How tiny the fingers and hands are. He hasn't come to dominate my life, but to accompany me and share everything he has with me. Love is all about sharing.

### Now I think about my own life:

- Where is the empty manger in me? Is it my loneliness, my pain, a weakness, a compulsion, an addiction?

- Might it be my boredom, my busyness?

- How about my anger, or my greed, or my selfishness?

- Or again, is it among the flat spots I find within myself? Is it depression, disillusionment, consumerism? Perhaps I have to fight black holes within myself such as grief or despondency.

- I begin to realize that if the emptiness is real for me, it is also real for Jesus: He wants to be there with me! He's waiting for my invitation: How about my asking him in?

- To ensure that he will come I need to do nothing but open the door of my heart.

I thank the shepherds for their presence and ask that I may go away from the scene as happy as they were. Finally, I review my prayer. As I end the retreat, I ask myself, "What would help me during Advent to open myself up more to the world of God?"

- Visiting a children's hospital?

- Attending a Carol Service or a performance of the *Messiah*?

- Acting as Santa Claus in a homeless center?

- Making a contribution to the Society of St. Vincent De Paul?

- Giving more time to Advent prayer?

- Encouraging a friend to visit the Sacred Space website?

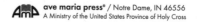